Verses In My Veins

Avni Siotia

India | USA | UK

Copyright © Avni Siotia
All Rights Reserved.

This book has been self-published with all reasonable efforts taken to make the material error-free by the author. No part of this book shall be used, reproduced in any manner whatsoever without written permission from the author, except in the case of brief quotations embodied in critical articles and reviews.

The Author of this book is solely responsible and liable for its content including but not limited to the views, representations, descriptions, statements, information, opinions, and references ["Content"]. The Content of this book shall not constitute or be construed or deemed to reflect the opinion or expression of the Publisher or Editor. Neither the Publisher nor Editor endorse or approve the Content of this book or guarantee the reliability, accuracy, or completeness of the Content published herein and do not make any representations or warranties of any kind, express or implied, including but not limited to the implied warranties of merchantability, fitness for a particular purpose.

The Publisher and Editor shall not be liable whatsoever...

Made with ❤ on the BookLeaf Publishing Platform
www.bookleafpub.in
www.bookleafpub.com

Dedication

To the people who make their love their home and end up homeless

This is for you

Preface

This book might *break you* in different ways

Acknowledgements

To my friends, thank you for listening to every version of the same story, for holding me through the heartbreak, and for reminding me I'm still whole even when I feel undone. You never got tired of me, even when I was tired of myself.

To my family, thank you for your quiet strength, your constant love, and for giving me the space to feel, write, and heal.
This book holds my heart.
It stands because of yours.

1. The First Glance

The first time I saw you, time forgot to move.
My heart skipped once—never found its groove.
The world slowed down, like it knew,
That I'd be standing still because of you.

Your laugh—too loud, too warm, too sweet,
I replayed it till it hurt to repeat.
You were a stranger, but something aligned,
A spark too soon, too undefined.

I watched the way your eyes would roam,
How every glance could make a home.
You looked too kind, too easy to want,
The kind of calm that hearts can't taunt.

They spoke to you, I turned away,
Jealous of what they got to say.
Their hands brushed yours, the crowd didn't mind—
And I just smiled, pretending I was fine.

It wasn't love, not then, not yet,
But something I can't quite forget.
A quiet pull, a gentle ache,

A dream I touch but never take.

So I hold my butterflies, fragile and tame,
A little envy, but no one to blame.
You don't know me, not even my name-
But still, you lit a lovely flame.

2. The Text I Never Meant to Send

I typed "hey," then erased it twice,
Why does something simple never feel right?
Swapped a smile for a dot instead—
God, why's this messing with my head?

Held my breath, hovered on send,
Like one click could make or end
The thousand thoughts inside my chest—
Do I seem calm, or just obsessed?

It's just a text, not love, not fate,
So why does my heart hesitate?
My thumb gave in, my fear was near,
But still... I wished that you were here.

Three dots. They danced, then died.
I stared, like hope was still implied.
Then boom—your name lit up the screen,
And suddenly, I forgot to breathe.

Your "hey" was simple, soft, and sweet,
But it hit like thunder in my seat.

You laughed at things that weren't that funny,
I melted when you called me "funny."

You said something dumb, I said "same,"
Smiling like the sound of my name
Was more than noise—it felt like start,
A tiny glow inside my heart.

Each text a spark I couldn't show,
You'll never guess how deep they go.
So there I sat, grinning like a fool,
Pretending not to care—God, I'm uncool.

But for once, I let it be,
Not perfect words, just honest me.
A tiny leap, a quiet bend—
And all because I clicked *send.*

3. What It Could Have Been

We said it wasn't a date, just a casual thing,
 A night out with friends—no meaning, no ring.
 But I still checked my hair three times,
 Picked my outfit like I was reading signs.

You texted, "On the way." I read it twice,
 Felt my stomach twist—God, this isn't right.
 Why does a group hang feel like a test?
 Why do I care if I look my best?

You walked in, wearing nothing new,
 But I swear the world just shifted hue.
 Everyone else began to blend,
 Except for you—my almost, my not-quite-end.

I watched you laugh with someone else,
 While I sat there, smiling by myself.
 We shared fries and tiny glances,
 I kept hoping for second chances.

You said, "Pass the drink." I passed my pride,
 Swallowed words I meant to hide.
 You teased me once, I laughed on cue,

But God, I just wanted to say, "I like you."

Our friends joked on; they didn't see
How close you stood next to me.
Your arm brushed mine—we didn't flinch,
But my chest still caved an inch.

You looked at me and smiled halfway,
And I carried that look the rest of the day.
A half-smile, a maybe, a spark so slight,
Enough to keep me up all night.

It wasn't a date—no hands were held,
No secret truths, no feelings spelled.
But when your laugh met mine mid-air,
It felt like something was *almost* there.

And maybe one day you'll look back too—
That night with friends, and me, and you.
But for now, I'll hold what I can take:
A memory dressed as a small heartbreak.

4. Love In Translation

We laughed like secrets shared at night,
 Your hand in mine—it felt so right.
 But *right* was never what we were,
 just blurred lines I couldn't deter.

You knew it too—how my voice would shake
 when I said your name, my calm would break.
 How my eyes stayed a beat too long,
 how every silence felt like a song.

I gave you poems shaped like sighs,
 You gave me smiles that felt like lies—
 not 'cause you meant them to deceive,
 But 'cause they made my heart believe.

I stayed your *person*, your *safe place*,
 But you never looked the other way.
 And every hug, though warm and true,
 carried the ache of not being you.

You held my heart like borrowed art,
 admired the strokes, but stayed apart.
 And I wish you'd felt it too—

The quiet storm I walked for you.

But some loves stay locked, unspoken, still;
Not every wish bends the world to will.
So I love you softly, from behind the light—
Your best friend always, almost... but not quite.

5. The One I Call Sunshine

I called you *sunshine* in my head,
  long before our names had met or spread.
  You walked in light, all golden glow,
  and smiled like you didn't even know.

You say the dumbest little things,
  and still, my chest grows fluttery wings.
  Your laugh's too loud, your jokes all lame—
  but somehow still, I blush the same.

I text you "lol," pretend I'm chill,
  while falling deeper against my will.
  You never see the mess you make—
  the breath you steal, the heart you shake.

You shine without a single try,
  like morning sun that floods the sky.
  And me? I melt but play the friend—
  your secret echo, till the end.

Some days I think, *just let him know,*
  but courage comes too soft, too slow.
  So I just grin when you're online,
  still call you mine—my sunshine.

6. The Space Between Us

I asked something small—nothing loud, nothing deep.
But still, your silence
cut me clean.
Like a truth you never meant to speak.

Left on *seen*.
And suddenly,
I'm not just quiet—I'm unwelcome.
Like a sound that lingers
after the song is done.

I re-read my text—ten times, maybe more,
checking if I came off wrong.
Or just too sore?

Maybe I laugh too long.
Or talk too fast.
Maybe I loved you too early.
Too vast.

Was I a glitch
in your peaceful scroll?
An echo you wish
you didn't know?

Because now every reply feels heavy and late,
like you're typing from habit,
not from fate.

You don't say it,
but I feel it
between your lines—
that I've become
one of your sighs.

And it hurts,
because I never meant
to weigh that much.

I only wanted
to be soft.
To be enough.

But here I am,
thinking of all the ways
I could be quieter, smaller,
less in the way.

Still typing a thousand things
I'll never send—
because you don't ghost me.

You just
end.

7. A Bridge Beneath The Dust

I don't know where we cracked—
If it were a word,
or something we lacked.

But I feel the gap
Every time I smile,
like laughter that doesn't
stretch the mile.

I miss you
in places no one sees,
in memories that cling
like autumn leaves.

And I know
I might've been wrong—
spoken too sharply,
held on too long.

So here it is—
not perfect, not clean,
but real, and shaking
in between:

I'm sorry.

For the things I said,
for what I broke,
for what you read.

I didn't mean
 to make you ache,
 to treat your softness
 like it wouldn't break.

You were home
 before I knew the word,
 And I ruined it
 with things unheard.

But if there's space
 left in your chest,
 even a corner—
 not the rest—

I'd still choose you,
 As my friend again,
 through all the silence,
 through all the *when*.

Because some bonds

are worth the mend,
and I don't want
a newer friend.

I want the one
 who saw me whole,
 before the cracks,
 before the cold.

So if there's still
 a chance for *us,*
 a tiny bridge
 beneath the dust,

I'll cross it slowly—
no pride, no plea,
 Just one question:

Will you still have me?

8. What We Saved

I didn't know how to start.
 So I held my breath,
 and handed you my heart.

A quiet *"sorry,"*—
 not grand, not neat,
 just shaking somewhere
 between my ribs and your feet.

You didn't flinch.
 You just looked away—
 like you'd been waiting
 for truth to finally
 sound my way.

We talked—finally.
 Not around it.
 Not beneath.
 Not pretending
 we were fine
 through gritted teeth.

We emptied the silence
 like pouring old tea—

bitter at first,
then somehow sweet.

You told me
where it hurt.
I told you
where I cracked.

And for once,
we didn't take
our love back.

We stitched the air
with what we lost,
with what we learned,
and what it cost.

No blame.
No fight.
Just two tired souls
trying to get it right.
Maybe it wasn't perfect.

But it was *real.*
And maybe that's
what healing feels like.

So here we are—
 not mending what broke,
 but learning the art
 of gentle hope.

Still soft.
 Still human.
 Still staying.

 For what we were
 was always
 worth saving.

9. The Colour In Us

I didn't plan to feel this way.
 But something in me slipped today.

You laughed with her—your eyes lit wide,
 and suddenly, something curled inside.

Not anger, no—just quiet ache,
 a tiny shift, a subtle break.
 A voice that whispered, *she gets to be*
 the close I dream for only me.

I watched you speak in softer tones,
 heard you laugh in ways unknown.
 The jokes I'd make, the looks we'd share—
 you gave them out like I wasn't there.

And god, I smiled. I played it fine.
 Said *"she's sweet,"* while swallowing mine.
 My voice stayed calm, my hands stayed still,
 but jealousy moved in
 against my will.

It wasn't rage. It wasn't spite.
 Just wanting what you gave her—light.

And wondering why I wasn't that,
the chosen seat, the chosen chat.

Maybe I don't have the right to say
I wish you'd only look my way.
But feelings grow in dim-lit rooms
where logic doesn't get a say.

So no, I didn't say a thing—
just let it burn beneath my skin.

My first real taste of feeling less,
of wanting more,
and getting *a guess.*

10. The Day That Isn't Mine

Your birthday's near, and I can't lie—
I smile too much and don't know why.
It's not my day—it's yours, I know,
but still, my pulse forgets to slow.

I count the days like fragile stars,
 each one holding what we aren't, what we are.
 You'll make a wish in golden light,
 and I'll fade softly out of sight.

I'll send a text—short, polite—
 You'll never know what it ignites.
 "Happy birthday :)"—that's all you'll see,
 But it carries too much heart from me.

I thought of gifts, of words to say,
 But silence felt the truest way.
 How do you wrap what's never named,
 a feeling soft, but unproclaimed?

I'll watch you laugh, the way you do—
 the kind that makes the room turn new.
 And I'll just stand there, half-alive,
 pretending distance can survive.

It isn't love, or maybe it is—
a quiet ache that feels like bliss.
A truth I hold, though never shown—
your day still feels
like mine alone.

11. The Quiet Kind of Love

It's 2 a.m. and your light's still on,
 Your notes are out, your focus long.
 You say, "I'm fine, just one more page,"
 But I can hear the tiredness cage.

So I stay up too, behind my screen,
 Typing *"You got this,"* trying to mean
 Every word like a soft embrace,
 For when the world forgets your face.

I can't solve math or write your line,
 But I can sit beside your grind.
 The silence hums, our chats slow down,
 But still, I'm here—though miles around.

And then it's me, on darker days,
 Lost in thought, in heavy haze.
 You send dumb memes, or simply say,
 "Still awake?"—and that's your way.

You don't fix it. You never try.
 You just stay. And that's why
 I hold you close, from far apart—
 You heal in ways that touch the heart.

We're not loud love, not wild flame,
We're quiet nights that feel the same.
We're late-night lamps and tired eyes,
Shared silence, steady compromise.

So read your books. I'll be right here.
You've got this love—my voice is near.
And when it's me who breaks in two,
I know you'll stay
Awake, too.

12. They Know Before I Do

My friends are tired—
They say your name before I do.
They finish my sentences,
Like loving you became theirs too.

"We know," they sigh,
"He texted," "He called."
They mock my grin,
But still catch me when I fall.

They roll their eyes,
When I bring you up again—
But they stay.
They listen.
They let me explain.

How your voice felt soft
Even through a screen,
How one small word
Can paint my day serene.

They say, "You're obsessed,"
And maybe it's true—
But they don't say it mean,

They say it the way people do
When they've seen you
Pull me back to life.

They hold my heart
When you forget to.
Their love is quiet,
But it sees me through.

They let me ramble,
They let me glow,
They see you
In every line I throw.

They sigh, "We're tired—
But God, you're happy."
And somehow that's enough
For them
To love you, too.

13. What My Heart Calls Love

This is my love—
 Not soft like stories,
 Not perfect, not neat.
 It spills, it aches,
 It drags its feet.

It isn't framed for strangers to see,
 No filters, no ease—
 Just the kind that stays
 Long after you leave.

I don't love in pieces.
 I don't play it safe.
 I love like the tide—
 Pulling even when it breaks.

Your words still echo
 When the room is still.
 I trace their ghosts
 Until they fill
 The parts of me
 You forgot to keep.

I write your name
 Where no one reads—
 In poems too quiet
 For anyone but me.

This is my love—
 Loud in all it doesn't do,
 Heavy in silence,
 Whole and true.

And I know—
 The world calls it "too much,"
 But I never learned
 How to dim my touch.

So I'll keep this love—
 Where it bruises, not bends,
 Where it hurts, but stays,
 And never pretends.

You may not choose it.
 You may not stay.
 But this is my love—
 And I give it anyway.

14. Almost Didn't Happen

I said it softly,
 Like the words might break.
 No armor, no act,
 Just my heart—bare, awake.

A quiet,
 "I like you,"
 No plan, no spin.
 Just me,
 And all the noise
 Caged within.

You blinked.
 And that was it—
 No smile,
 No sound.
 Just silence,
 And me trying not to drown.

So I laughed it off,
 Said, "Forget it, I'm dumb,"
 Like it was nothing—
 Like I hadn't gone numb.

Like my chest didn't burn,
 Like I wasn't shaking,
 Like my world didn't tilt
 For the love I was faking.

And you—
 You looked at me slowly.
 And I swore that was it—
 The quiet rejection,
 The final hit.

But then you said it,
 Soft, unsure,
 Like the words themselves
 Weren't pure.

"I like you too."
 Just that.
 No fireworks,
 No song.
 Just truth,
 Finally belonging.

And suddenly,
 Every heartbreak I'd rehearsed
 Felt wrong.

Because here we were—
 Not perfect, not planned,
 But real,
 And trembling,
 Hand in hand.

Two hearts,
 One pause,
 And a breath between—
 A love
 That almost
 Went unseen.

15. The Night Didn't End, It Just Slept

It started with,
 "Just five more minutes,"
 But five became
 Midnight digits.

You on your screen,
 Me on mine—
 Yawning through
 Each blurry line.

I watched you talk,
 Then slow your pace,
 Eyes half-closed,
 Soft on your face.

We didn't say much
 After two a.m.,
 But somehow silence
 Felt like a gem.

You laughed,
 I smiled,
 You blinked too slow—

And I knew
It was time
To let it go.

But neither of us
 Pressed the red.
 You curled up,
 I lay in bed.

"Are you asleep?"
 I whispered low.
 You didn't answer—
 God, I hope so.

Because something about
 That quiet grace,
 The trust it takes
 To fall—
 Right in front of my face—

Felt warmer than
 Anything you said,
 As your screen still lit
 The side of your bed.

And maybe that's love,
 Or almost, at least—

Not kisses, not plans,
Just peace
Upon peace.

So we stayed
Until sleep,
No goodbyes,
No plan—
Just me,
Just you,
And the hum
Of the fan.

16. In the Shade of Fire

I thought love
 Would feel like light—
 Warmth in the morning,
 Soft and right.

But then came you—
 And it wasn't soft.
 It was wild;
 It was loud.
 It burned,
 And it never turned off.

You weren't calm.
 You were fire in disguise—
 A touch that trembled,
 A look that pried.
 And I,
 Who once wanted
 Quiet skies,
 Fell for the chaos
 In your storming eyes.

Love wasn't pastel
 When it came to you.

It was red—
 Sharp.
 Bleeding.
 True.

It stained my hands,
 It broke my sleep.
 It made me feel
 Far too deep.

But God—
 We loved the red,
 Didn't we?
 The crash,
 The rush,
 The way we'd breathe
 Like the world could split
 And we'd still kiss
 In the heat
 Of it.

And maybe it hurt,
 And maybe it bled,
 But I'd do it again—

17. Jealousy, Quietly Human

It caught me off guard—
The way his jaw clenched,
The shift in his tone,
The way he flinched
When I laughed
At someone else's joke—
A little too long,
A little too soft.

He didn't say much,
Just looked away,
But God—
His silence
Said everything
He wouldn't say.

And I wanted to ask,
"Is it jealousy?"

But I didn't.
I just smiled,
Pretending I didn't notice
His hands go still,
His voice drop low,

His eyes trace
What he didn't want to know.

Because I know that feeling—
I've lived in it.
I've scrolled through chats,
Read too much into it.
I've felt that ache
When he talked to her;
When I faded out
And the center blurred.

But seeing it now,
From the other side—
His breath held tight,
His pride half-tied—
Something in me
Softened slow.
A kind of warmth
I didn't know
I needed
Until I saw
He needs it too.

And maybe he'll never say,
"You're mine,"
But I read it

Between every line—

In the way he cared,
In the way he stayed,
In the look that said
He'd push the world away
If it ever made me
Look at someone
The way I look at him.

And for once—
I wasn't the only one
Who felt too much
And said too little.

18. Where Something Began

I got ready
 Like it mattered—
 Like he'd notice
 Every strand out of place,
 Every second I spent
 Fixing my face.

And maybe he didn't.
 Maybe he just smiled,
 Said, "You look nice,"
 In that calm, boyish style.
 But it was enough
 To make my pulse race—
 God, what do I even say?
 When did I start
 Liking his face?

The table was small,
 Our hands were close.
 We talked like friends,
 But I felt it most
 In the quiet breaks,
 When he looked at me—
 Like I was something

He couldn't quite believe.

I laughed too loudly.
He tapped his glass.
He teased me once,
I let it pass.

But the butterflies
Weren't shy tonight—
They fluttered wild
Each time he looked right.

And no,
There was no kiss,
No dramatic scene,
No fireworks
Like in silver screens.
But he walked me home,
His steps in line,
And said, "This was good—
Let's do it another time."

And I said yes,
But what I meant was more.
More of you.
More of this.
More of whatever

We're headed for.

Because tonight felt
 Like something new—
 The first time
 It was just
 Us two.

19. Ours Didn't End in Hate

Not every story
 Ends in smiles.
 Some stop halfway,
 After too many miles.

No one yelled.
 No one lied.
 No one left
 Because love had died.

It wasn't cold.
 It wasn't cruel.
 We didn't play games.
 We didn't break the rules.

We just looked
 At the same sky—
 From two places
 Too far, too wide.

And the silence grew
 Where our plans had been,
 Like love was strong,
 But fate didn't let it win.

People think endings
 Come with blame—
 That someone walks off,
 Or says the wrong name.

But ours?
 Ours was soft.
 It cracked, not burned.
 We held the love,
 But had to return it.

 To the place
 Where it began—
 Unfinished hearts,
 Unwritten plans.

 And maybe
  That's the hardest kind:
  To still want
  What you had to leave behind.

 To still feel
  What you're told to forget.
  To still call it love
  Without regret.

Because it was love.
 Still is, I swear.
 Just not a love
 That life could spare.

And while most stories
 End with goodbye,
 Ours ends in—
 We never got to try.

20. It's Been A Month?

It's been a month
 Since you stopped checking in.
 Since my phone stayed dry,
 Since silence began to win.

No texts,
 No late-night calls.
 Just me—
 And four blank walls.

They say
 "No contact helps you heal."
 But all it's done
 Is make this real.

Because now it's not a fight,
 Not a phase,
 Not a rough night—
 It's a routine,
 Of you not being mine,
 Of me pretending
 I'm just fine.

But I'm not.

I'm tired of lying.
 Tired of pretending
 I'm still trying—
 To find your name
 In every screen,
 To unfeel
 Everything you still mean.

I've deleted photos,
 But kept the pain.
 Buried your laughter,
 But hear it again.

And God,
 If silence is peace,
 Why am I breaking
 Piece by piece?

I don't even know
 What I'd say
 If you came back—
 If you ever make
 Your way
 Back to me.

Maybe nothing.
 Maybe everything.

Maybe just—
"Where the hell have you been?"

Because I've been here,
 One month in,
 And somehow
 Still losing
 A love
 I've already lost.

21. If This Is the End

If this is the end,
  Let it be quiet.
  No last fight,
  No blame,
  No riot.

Just you there,
  And me here—
  Still loving,
  Still unclear.

Because no one ever
  Taught me how
  To carry love
  That isn't mine now.

I don't know
  How to unfurl your name,
  How to walk away
  And not feel the same.

You were the beginning—
  Of poems,
  Of light,

Of everything soft
That once felt right.

And now you're the ending,
Too soon, too rough—
The story that stopped
While we still had
Enough.

They say I'll love again.
But they don't get it—
How do you replace
A heart
Where his fingerprints
Still sit?

How do I smile
At a brand-new start,
When he is still alive
In the back of my heart?

And maybe one day
You'll find this page.
Maybe years will pass,
And we'll both have aged.

But I'll still be me—

Soft,
And true.
The kind of love
That never outgrew
You.

So if this is forever,
And if we don't meet again,
Just know—
I loved you
Until the very end.

And if there's a future
Where fate is kind,
I hope we find
What we lost in time.

But for now,
This is where I leave it be.
No happy ending.
Just—

"You'll always mean everything to me."

www.ingramcontent.com/pod-product-compliance
Lightning Source LLC
Chambersburg PA
CBHW070458050426
42449CB00012B/3025